BRAZEN

OTHER BOOKS BY ALEXIS RHONE FANCHER

How I Lost My Virginity to Michael Cohen &
other heart stab poems (Sybaritic Press, 2014)

State of Grace: The Joshua Elegies (KYSO Flash Press, 2015)

Enter Here (KYSO Flash Press, 2017)

Junkie Wife (Moon Tide Press, 2018)

The Dead Kid Poems (KYSO Flash Press, 2019)

EROTIC: New & Selected (NYQ Books, 2021)

DUETS (Small Harbor Press, 2022) with Cynthia Atkins

Stiletto Killer (Edizione Italia, Roma 2022)

BRAZEN

ALEXIS RHONE FANCHER

To Seely
with love
Alexis Rhone Fancher
3/31/23

NQY Books™

The New York Quarterly Foundation, Inc.
Beacon, New York

NYQ Books™ is an imprint of The New York Quarterly Foundation, Inc.

The New York Quarterly Foundation, Inc.
P. O. Box 470
Beacon, NY 12508

www.nyq.org

First Edition

Set in New Baskerville

Layout by Raymond P. Hammond

Cover Design and Photo by Alexis Rhone Fancher

Library of Congress Control Number: 2023932276

ISBN: 978-1-63045-084-7

For Mark and Sheila Marion, with love.

CONTENTS

BRAZEN

Why We Didn't

At the beach in late August, deep in the leather bucket seats of his 289 Mustang, we didn't, although he kissed me with tongue and open mouth. We didn't, although his finger traced my nipples to pinpoints on the outside of my blouse, and his hot breath seared my neck. His hands stayed reluctantly above my waist. I wanted to pull him into me, a vortex, his tongue so deep in my throat it disappeared. On the beach in Malibu, he didn't, although he tongued the hollow of my throat, followed it down to my aching-to-be-fondled breasts, and stopped cold. On the hood of his car, he didn't, when he bent me back against the still-warm metal, and covered my body with his. We didn't, but I rubbed the hard swell of his penis through the prophylactic of his jeans, ground myself into him like I knew what I was doing, and I wanted him to do it, too. Before he left for college in San Diego, he didn't; he left me behind in L.A. I was sixteen, eager as fuck. He'd just turned eighteen. And when his father warned him, *Eighteen into sixteen don't go,* he listened.

Tonight at last call, J. calls me his Brown Liquor Girl again,

his voice dark urgency, like when we were attached.

I let him grip my hips, slow dance me back to that lust,

to the parking lot, his car,
my tube top a trophy in one hand,

a bottle of Southern Comfort in his other.
He pours that sweet Joplin down my throat,

guides my hand between his legs.
Drives

to the Malibu motel with ocean views,
vibrating beds, and once more, our delicious thrashing,

complimentary KY where the Gideon should be,
the insomniac waves rocking us long before my marriage,

and now after.

When I ask him which part of me he loves best,
J. answers: *What's missing*,

tonguing the place where my nipple had been.
He doesn't mind the mastectomy scar,

the one my husband can't bring himself to touch.

Midnight in the Backyard of Lust and Longing

The sapphists are at it again. *Screw you's!* ricochet off our common walls, invectives landmine my window. *You cheating bitch!* Like clockwork, this drunken Friday night climax to their ceaseless lovers' quarrel. *I'll kill you!* I hear the big one growl. And then the smashed plates, the screams. By the time the cops arrive it's a full-out brawl, the two women spilling from their back door, tussling across the no man's land between their tiny backyard and mine. Worse than animals. This time it's Holly, the younger one, dragged to the patrol car, yellow hair wilding, small hands cuffed behind her back, kicking at the cops in those Daisy Dukes, an army jacket waifing her silhouette. More clothes than she had on the last time the cops rolled up. Or the time before. It's almost dawn, and the trees shiver in the fog, raccoons slink through the tall grass. Marie, Holly's better half, paces the yard in a blue bathrobe and slippers, smoking a cigarette, sobbing as the cops jam her lover into their car. *Watch her head!* she cries, and flings herself across the yard, lunges for Holly through the glass. *Baby! Baby!* she sobs, the reason for their discord forgotten. Holly mouths a sloppy kiss. Marie opens her robe, presses herself against the glass. Can you believe it? I would give anything to be loved like that.

After the Restraining Order Expires, M. Begs Me
to Meet Him for Lunch

Says he "killed it" in anger management class,
that everything's under control. Bygones.

I drink my unrequited malice.
Wonder how soon he'll turn deadly.

You're a sip, he says, *barely a swallow.*
He laps up my resistance,

leans over, nuzzles my neck,
wraps his arm around my indecision.

Remind me again why we broke up?
He was always a fine interrogator.

I watch his shirt ride up above his belly,
where I'd lay my head to suck him off.

The desperation of his stark, white skin,
the crude exposure.

I'd pull his shirt back down,
but it would be too much like tenderness.

Grab Shot

You Ferrari baby. You Lotus Elan. You dream man. Smooth moves, always some sleek bitch on your arm, and me side-kickin', just afterthought. So I shoot you, replicate you in oversized prints spread out on my bed like facsimile. Those blown-up biceps, fine-tuned torso, face up on my pillow, your perfect pores. How the camera loves you, baby, those smoldering, Billy Dee shots aimed straight at a woman's vulnerability. How you juice them, seduce them, your voice dropping an octave when a woman calls. And you get all Barry White. You've kept up the upkeep. Changed the oil. Sleek. Toned. You Alfa *and* Romeo, baby. You candy apple. You metal fleck. The wind buffs glitter all around you. That night at my studio after one too many Hennessys, we stand toe to toe and I turn my lips to yours, ask, *why not me?* You grab my ass with two hands, squeeze, and shrug. *Baby got no back.* And I flash to that chorus line of sloe-eyed beauties you've bedded, each one bottom-heavy, riper than I could ever be. As if derrière were the measure of a woman. *Let's get back to work,* you say. You rev up your engine. I flick on the lights. Oh, baby, you shimmer, you gleam. *Stand up,* I tell you. *Pull the shirt above your head.* Now you can't see me for real. You, who can't see the Beemers for the beaters. You, who wouldn't know love if it bit you on the ass.

Last Night on the Nature Channel We See Each Other for Who We Really Are

1. *Varanus komodoensis*:

Watch the Komodo dragon swallow a monkey in increments,
and tell me you're unchanged. I dare you.

It feels familiar, but it could be a dream.
The bottom half, floppy, long tail and hind legs all loosey-goosey.

Like me, bandy-legged, woozy after you've worked your lingual magic.
Poor monkey! You used to say, only you meant me.

I've seen objects disappear inside *your* mouth, remember?
I get excited just thinking about it.

2. *Draco viridi luscus*:

I'm trying hard to give you another chance, but that green-eyed dragon
has taught me to expect the worst. Already I'm feeling at loose ends,
swallowed up.

You're on your best behavior until you're not.

Dusk finds the crows still raucous, flying circles around us.
The old tom yowls a horny duet, his one good eye on the lookout.

The Famous Poet Skates in Perpetuity

My high school sweetheart
gave me irises
the first time we fucked.

My friend's first lover
gave her herpes.

A famous poet,
he made her think
she invented lust,

counted on her discretion,
taught her to be loyal as a dove.

Even after her diagnosis,
his sin lives forever
in her secret mouth.

Even now,
she refuses to name him.

When your stepdaughter warns you not to let her roommate's cat escape...

it's like she has a premonition.

After she leaves, you'll explore her off-campus apartment,
snoop in her drawers, try on her graduation cap.

You will smoke her dope & drink her last Bud Light.
The two of you have never been close.

You'll read the roommate's diary, take notes.

The cat, a tom of indeterminate age,
will rub his thin, orange body against your ankles.

You'll walk into the bathroom to pee,
gag at the litter box teeming with hardened turds,
avoid the ones on the floor.

The ammonia of cat piss mixed with
the unmistakable scent of soiled Kotex
will leak into the hall

where it will mingle with four-day-old Mexican food
and pizza stuck on plates in the kitchen.

You'll recall your stepdaughter's slovenly ways,
how badly she treated you,
how relieved you were when she left home.

The cat will pace, yowling at the bathroom door like Tom Petty.
But when you put him in the litter box, he'll balk, stare up at you
with marmalade eyes, nudge you toward the front door.

It will be an act of mercy.

Later, you will sit on the stained couch
where you'll watch reruns of *Forensic Files* in the fading light,
and wait for your stepdaughter's return.

Then you will deny everything.

Power Play

When my lover tells me I cannot say *no,* and I protest, she parts my legs, says *yes, baby. Yes.* I do what I'm told. *No* becomes a foreign country. I take it as permission. Open season. So when the waiter asks if there'll be anything else, I peruse his menu. I'm stuffed, but I say *yes,* cram my mouth with macaroons and chocolate. And when the Lyft driver seduces me in the rear-view, eyes me like prey, asks, *May I kiss you?* I say *yes.* And when the long-legged woman I've long lusted after at the gym wonders aloud if I'm single, asks me to dinner and a movie, I say *yes.* And when she invites me into her bed, what can I say but *yes, yes, yes?* And when my fan in Nova Scotia begs me to be his muse, to sanction an explicit ode to my breasts, my ankles, my lower lip, a poem he'd never show his wife, I cannot say *no* to his lust and delusion. Now he wants to climb me, sublime me, shoot me full of stars. *Is this what you want, too?* he writes, and I answer *yes.* And when I return to my lover at last and she sinks into the heady dampness between my thighs, looks up at me and asks, *Have you been faithful?* I say, *Yes.*

Hey, 19: Daddy's Pal Paul and I Cut to the Chase

Paul pushes into me with all the desperation of his 45 years. *Hey, 19,* he moans, like the song, and I smile, murmur encouragement as he ruts and grunts, his beer belly slapping against my ass. I've cured him forever, he says, of loving Ann; says I'm a better fuck than his ex-wife ever was, that she never could give a proper blow job, and did I think I could I love an older man, and did I think my daddy would mind? Have to confess, the dude's got moves. He's doing things to me *down there* that thrill my nubile heart. That's when I remember Paul's a gynecologist. I figure I could do worse, given my run of bad luck with boys my age, and that doomed foray into lesbo-land with my crazy girlfriend, Anjelica. *I'm all in,* I tell Paul, and Mona Lisa all over the place, wearing only a smile as I languish on the bed at the Palm Springs Hotel, and fall in love...with room service. I run up quite a bill: Dom Perignon, Beluga caviar on Ritz crackers, a giant-sized box of Jujubes. And when Paul gets back from the jewelry shop in the Arcade with the small blue box that sparkles, the last thing I want is for the evening to end, for him to come to his senses.

At the Party, the Famous Poet Goes Too Far with the Latest Sweet Young Thang

Baby, you were a tiger last night,
the famous poet growls,
paws at my breast like an apology.

He knows I like it rough.

I know his penchant for variety,
his lust's juvenescence.

I saw his arm
slip around her flirtation,
saw him meet her platinum gaze,

maneuver her out on the deck,
grope her like he once groped me.

When we make our make-up love,
I picture impossibly young women,
lined up, his for the taking,

and I hear my time running out,
that desperate, loudening thrum.

I'm his blond, his punch-drunk muse.
He knows I'll go down swinging.

Old School

—as told to the poet by SGM

It's 1984. A board member at the L.A. Library Association pushes me against the Xerox machine, forces his tongue down my throat.

It's 1977 when I watch the musical director at Lincoln Center jack off under his desk. Over dirty martinis his assistant confides it's her job to wipe up the semen splatter each night before she goes home.

It's 1985. I'm raising money for medical research when Dr. Abdul R.H. greets me at the Saudi embassy. When my shoe catches the hem of my dress, exposing my breasts, he claps.

It's 1978. The Brooklyn Academy of Music. Six of us girls lunch at my boss's flat in the Village. Before dessert he leans back, unzips his fly.

It's 1988. My boss, notorious ladies' man James "Jimmy" R., president of Cal State L.A., propositions me, my sister, and every woman under the age of thirty. Afraid of retribution, no one reports him.

It's 1971. Six of us cheerleaders at Blair High watch a man in the stands masturbate to our practice routines. I've never seen a penis, up close, erect. *What 'cha lookin' at?* he smirks.

It's 1985. Board member David M. asks me out in front of the entire board. His masculinity's at stake.

It's 1986. Dr. Abdul R.H. invites me to discuss the research budget at his L.A. hotel. His suite is filled with roses. He's naked under the robe.

It's 1972. Dr. Lusk, university physician, palpates my breasts as part of a sore throat exam. *You have nice, German breasts,* he exclaims. He prescribes a spanking, lozenges.

It's 1973. Danny hits me in the face for calling him a male chauvinist pig. Later, he holds me outside of a moving car until I agree to fuck him.

It's 1978. I tell the president of the Brooklyn Academy of Music we're all resigning as a group. *Who is "we"?* he asks. I realize I'm on my own.

Thirst

1. Like my love life, L.A. is in a perpetual state of drought.

It's a crime to water the lawn.

2. Rumors of coyotes overrun the neighborhood.

When they lose their fear of humans, they mingle,
associate people with food, water.

3. My cat's photo is on a milk carton.

The scattered remains of lost lovers and household pets
litter my dreams.

4. *Coyotes have rights, too,* my neighbor says,
when I complain about the carnage. His Chihuahua's leash
hangs on the door.

5. When the famous poet arrived from West Virginia, stood at our sink,
soaped his hands over and over, water gushing out of the tap,
I kept quiet as long as I could.

This is L.A., for fuck's sake, I said at last.

6. The white, alpha dog next door is silent for once,
his cohort, the yappy Dachshund, strangely missing.

7. The last time I bathed without guilt, in a full tub of water,
the century had just turned.

When My Son Is Two Weeks Old, Yvonne Gives Me
a Massage

1. After his birth,
milk whirlpools my body,
centrifugal force
a seductive tug at my uterus.

Orgasmic, the rhythm and pull
of his suckling. I, besotted.
Devoured.

2. With me prone on the slim table,
Yvonne oils my back, massages the ache
—those bra straps dug into my shoulder blades—
her slippery hands hot, reverent.

She looks at me like my son does,
famished.

Her fingers flip the same switch
that primes my pump;
oxytocin floods my body.
I dampen.

And when she turns me on my back,
milk auto-pilots from my breasts.
I am leaking.

3. Yvonne, who is barren,
moans as breast milk splashes
on the terrazzo floor.

I see my reflection
through her surprise:

pleasure bubbling over
like a fountain.

For Mary, My College Roommate, Who Sells Drugs & Wants to Be a Porn Star

1. The Movie

Take off your clothes or get out! the director shouts.
You're entering my set!
I thought I was entering my apartment.

I traverse a writhing girl, trip over her muscular,
long-haired lover. Mary waves from our sofa. She's naked,
except for a glittering tiara.
A man's head emerges from between her thighs.

Hungry, I head for the kitchen.

When I grab a jar of Nutella from the 'fridge,
the director is behind me, still shooting.

We'll film it, he says.
You could smear the stuff all over you.
Mary could lick it off.

2. Mary's boyfriend, Ron,

breaks into the bathroom while I shower.
He reaches through the curtain,
offers to scrub my back.

I offer to call the cops.

While my roommate sleeps,
Ron slithers between my sheets,
his snake dick seeking me out like prey.

What will Mary say? I ask.
Ron shrugs. *Who's going to tell her?*

3. The next day

I slide open the door of my closet:
floor to ceiling bricks of marijuana,
pungent and penitentiary-worthy,
wall in my wardrobe.

Don't worry, Mary promises.
It'll all be gone in the morning.

The Famous Poet Asks Me for Naked Photos

1. *You are a forbidden planet,*
he says at the bar after his reading,
when all the hangers-on have gone.

He drains his third martini.

I smile.

Encouraged, he puts his arm
around my shoulder, confesses
he can jack off to a photo only once;
he needs a constant supply.

2. The famous poet smells
musty, shopworn. He pops a breath mint,
runs a hand through his silver mane.

You are my muse and savior, he says,
right after he tells me his second wife
no longer likes sex.

He smoothes an aberrant bang
from my forehead.
Are you clean-shaven? he asks,
staring at the mystery between my thighs.
Or do you roll au naturelle?

3. The famous poet wants me
to take a selfie in the ladies' room,
pull my skirt up and my panties
down, and I admit, it gets me wet.
Like him, I'm not getting any at home.
I want to wrap my legs around his head.

4. The famous poet swears his wife
is cool with his serial betrayals,
that they inhabit different countries
in the same, small house.

But I've seen his wife at parties, how
his philandering makes her flinch,
the face of desperation, choked down,
Sylvia Plath style.

The face that wants me to suffocate
like Sylvia did

and watch. The face that says,
once I was you.

She Says Stalker/He Says Fan

If you can't be free, be a mystery.
—Rita Dove, "Canary"

She's a singed torch song, a broken chord, the slip-shadow between superstar and the door. She's that long stretch of longing riding shotgun from nowhere to L.A., a bottle of Jack Daniels snug between her thighs, always some fresh loser at the wheel. She's the Zippo in your darkness, a glimmer of goddess in your god-forsaken life, her voice a rasp, a whisky-tinged caress. She *gets* you, and you know the words to all her songs, follow her from dive bar to third-rate club clapping too loudly, making sure she makes it home. She's as luckless in love as you are, star-crossed, the pair of you (in your dreams). If only we could choose who we love! Tonight the bartender pours your obsession one on the house, dims the lights in the half-empty room as she walks on stage, defenseless, but for that 0018 rosewood Martin she cradles in her lap like a child. If you ask nicely, she'll end with the song you request night after night, about the perils of unrequited love. You'll blurt out your worship into her deaf ear, while her fingers strum your forearm and her nails break your skin. *Give the lady whatever she wants,* you'll tell the barkeep. Like that's even possible.

34

Poem for the Girl Who Wanted to Stop Time

when the sirens made apartment dogs keen,
she howled for him—her body a longing
                                        she gave away all her clothes
                                        she knew no one could love her

                        because he danced solo
                        because she flew planes into mountains
                        because she circled the drain

her Scorpio was in Venus; he'd left his in a stranger's bed.
                                        she needed what was left of him
                                        it was an inside job

he wanted too much   he didn't come home
he couldn't choose   he hated silence
                                        he couldn't love

                        because she lived in the outfield
                        because he feared the dark
the trees were crying
                        she stumbled and fell
she couldn't take it
back
                before she knew it, the stars had misaligned
                        the moon was in Paris
                        the astrologer smelled of beer
she'd lie if questioned
she knew the ropes

she ate like a bird   the shoes pinched
the ocean waved   he left her stranded
the clock stopped   she wanted to die
he always left
she always forgave him

                                        now that he was dead
                                        and that girl had disappeared.

Pas de Deux

1. She said: *Tell me one thing that doesn't end badly?*

2. I wanted her ruffled tutu and toe shoes,
pink satin ribbons latticed up my legs like body armor.

She knew I avoided mirrors, reflecting pools.
What, she asked, *do you dislike about your face?*

3. Hers was a thoughtless beauty,
while I worked hard for everything,

danced my body into submission,
those endless practice hours at the barre,
legs turned out, toes pointing, pointing.

4. *La laisse tomber,* she said, when I leapt,
head-first into her arms. She let me fall.

5. I dreamed a solo, spotlight, applause,
not tucked in the corps de ballet.

She, too, dreamed prima ballerina. On stage,
her wicked tour jetés just missed my face.

6. *A dancer in love with anyone but herself
is called an understudy,*
she laughed when I asked her to choose.

That night, I arabesqued right through her;
she tasted jealousy for the first time.

7. She became a self-fulfilling prophecy,
out till dawn, sex-soaked, sweaty with another,
less ambitious girl's perfume. (See #1).

8. When I found the photos with my eyes x'ed out,
I knew I would leave her.

My eyes—my one good feature.

I Audition for the Belly Dancer Job While My Pure-bred Siamese Lily Gets Laid

I gyrate like Little Egypt in my harem pants and diaphanous veil.
The lessons with Fatima have paid off.

But it's the minefield between the restaurant's bar and the stage.
Barefoot, my limp is even more pronounced.

Last night I watched two cats humping.
One of them was mine. Like me, she's been in an accident.

Like me, her bum leg makes her an easy target.

Do you have any scars? the manager asks.
No, I lie...worthless.

The tomcat's claws draw blood when I yank the lovers apart.
Bad girl! I hiss, though it's not Lily's fault.

Do you have a drinking problem? Take drugs?
I shake my head.

Like I must be damaged to work here.

I won't judge you, the manager promises,
I'm on everything but roller-skates.

My Body Is a Map of Scars

A girl with good legs wears dresses, my blind date sighs over dinner.

My body is a minefield. My body is liability, is albatross.

The gash across my eyebrow where nothing grows.
The crisscross that mars my rebuilt leg;
how full-length mirrors avoid me.

I chew prime rib thoughtfully, make two trips to the salad bar on
my ugly legs.

My body is betrayal. My body is stain, is renegade.

The sad limp. The gouge at the base of my throat.

I order an after-dinner cognac. Then another.

My body is car crash. My body is plunder.

My body/Not my body.

I watch his eyes disappear into the long-legged perfection of a girl
in a tiny skirt, the green of a ripe avocado.

No lattice-laced scars furrow *her* past and future.

I dream a lover blind to trauma.

Look at my palm: see how the lifeline ends and then restarts?

For the Russian Waitress at the Yorkshire Grill
Who Reads Akhmatova on Her Break

She's a sloe-eyed Madonna in a black uniform, refilling napkin
holders, topping off salt shakers, funneling ketchup from one half-
full bottle to another. I, among the faithful, come to worship at her
station, always sitting in her section. I'm convinced she's secretly
the Virgin of Feodorovskaya, venerated icon of the upper Volga,
the way she must have looked first thing in the morning, brewing
coffee, sans Byzantine jewels and heavy crown.

She's the patron saint of diners, the dispenser of special orders
shimmering behind the counter, a saint tethered to the linoleum
by tired booths and chipped Formica. When she takes my order, I
bow my head, genuflect; her tangled, familiar accent a benediction.
When she sees me eye her worn paperback, peeking out of her
pocket, *The Complete Poems of Anna Akhmatova*, she fingers the
author's cover photo with reverence.

I want to remove the pins from her hair, loosen the tight bun, let
the blunt wisps fall to her chin, narrowing her high-cheekboned
visage. I want to worship at the pout of her lips, nuzzle at her neck's
altar. I want to slip her uniform off her shoulders, bury myself in
her Russian-ness, pull her down next to me in the booth, feed her
bits of brisket, dill pickle, baklava, give her sips of my tea.

You're beautiful! I'll tell her, but she'll shake her head. She has no
faith in platitudes. I'll take her photo when she's not looking. Print
it as proof of faith, an 8x10 glossy, then bring it to her, an offering.
I, too, am Russian (on my father's side), I'll say. *I, too, carry Akhmatova in
my pocket.*

It will be the first time I've seen her smile.

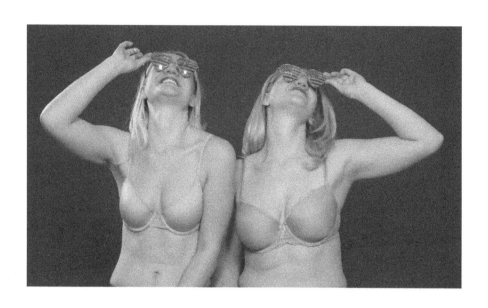

Target Practice

When the former football star and his entourage leave a $1 tip for me on the table, I run after him shouting, *Mr. Olsen! Merlin Olsen! You forgot your fucking dollar!*

Phone sex proves far more lucrative, but isolating. My neighborhood turns dangerous. The landlord bars the windows.

I consider rescuing a pit bull, but let my ex move in instead, sleep on my couch.

He brings chef's knives, a sour dough starter, and his Glock 17.

Does phone sex with strangers turn you on? he soon asks, but not in a good way.

Everything sets him off: murmurs, screams—pitched beyond normal hearing.

Tamales! Tamales! the street vendor shouts every Tuesday and Thursday afternoon. *The next time I want dinner made in someone's bathtub,* my ex says, *I'll let you know.*

He teaches me to grill chicken, lamb chops, beef kabobs. The Croatian butcher on 25th Street becomes his best friend.

Sometimes my ex comes home with blood on his shirt.

How rough do you want it today, baby? I say into the cold phone. I now have a stable of regulars.

At the gun range, I fire an entire clip into the target's center. My ex is impressed.

You just blow me away. It's the nicest thing he's said in years.

I tell him that night he can sleep in my bed, that he can fuck me, if he can find a pulse.

The Famous Poet Sexts Me While His Wife's Asleep

Bad boy poets thirst for love, too.
He pretends it's a joke, but it's not.

When he needs quenching, he turns to me.

As always, he lies on his side of the bed, pajamas
unbuttoned, hunched over the phone so wifey can't see the glow.

She'd hate to see him happy,
hard cock straining against his fly.

What are you wearing?

I'm not. I fire off a selfie; I can almost hear him moan.

You light me up.

I tell myself not everyone's a famous poet's muse.
Even if that bad boy's over 70.

Tonight he wants narrative; I stoke his dreams,
tell him what every man wants to hear, how huge he feels

between my thighs, how I burn for his touch.

When he ignites, he's nineteen again, or even forty,
not this aging poet, jacking off

to a girl he should pay by the hour.

That one time we met, he smelled like bonfire,
his bones, brittle kindling, blue eyes aflame.

And I, who sleep solo, wait for his texts.

Smoke signals on a desiccated highway.
Until I light the match.

43

Sweet Tooth

The man in the window is cheesecake;
if I could soar across Main Street
and land in his arms, I'd eat him for dessert.

He's caramel poured in those low-slung jeans,
a Sugar Daddy™ ("lasts forever if you lick it right").

He's marzipan, clean-cut, the jut of his hipbone
reflecting the sun. I'm come undone

by the clockwork of his days,
his devil's food dismount from that Shimano aluminum bike,
how he disappears inside the foyer.

If he were mine,
I'd ride him like a stolen bicycle.

He strips down to sweetmeat, Monday through Friday, 5 p.m.
"Happy Hour," when he hangs

the bike on the wall.
And me, happy to watch his muscles ripple.

He stretches out on the bed, my creature of habit,
his O'Henry™ straining against its wrapper.

This I know:
He's an all-day sucker.
He doesn't believe in drapes.

When I asked him to turn me on he said:

—*for Michael Cohen*

1. *Turn yourself on.*
His voice had that flat affect lovers get
when they're done with you.

2. *You're burning through men,* my mother warned.
Like there was a limit.

Every day, a fresh opportunity
to ruin some poor man's life.

I was on fire.

3. *I'd take a bullet for you,* he told me once.
And meant it.

I didn't answer.
I tasted loneliness at last.

4. And he, behind me,
palms on my ass, riding.

5. (That night) I fell asleep with the TV remote
between my legs.

When I awoke, he was gone.

6. If he knew what I would write about him,
he'd have hated me sooner.

7. Sometimes, the person you'd take a bullet for
is the one behind the gun.

After the breakup, I retreat into Sappho at my usual diner

Beneath crusty topping, the cheddar and noodles—a long blonde hair. This is no accident. It's a call for help, and me, too morose to hear. The long, blonde waitress reads over my shoulder, waits for my credit card, plays with her split ends. She points at my book, asks, *Who's Sappho?* When I tell her, *a poet from ancient Greece,* she rolls her eyes. *Me? I like noir. Ever read any Elmore Leonard? Jim Thompson?* she asks. *The Killer Inside Me?* She attacks the crumbs on my table. I'm not sure what she wants. *Is that what you've got?* I ask her. *A killer inside you?* The waitress shrugs. *Don't we all?* She strikes too close to home. When I don't answer, she tries again. *Maybe you should be reading something relevant, writing about, fuck, I dunno, slow death at a greasy spoon?* When I look surprised, she gets in my face. *I see you here, every day, same table, writing in that notebook, always alone. What? Real life's too real for ya? Gotta retreat to ancient history?* She's got my number. The waitress picks up my plate. *Jim Thompson'd tell you, women are like crockery. Chipped,* she says. *Disposable. Even your precious Sappho.* She points at the glistening fat beading off my abandoned mac and cheese. *Greece? I'll show you ancient grease.* She palms my credit card, brings it to the cashier. *Who broke you?* I ask, when she returns with my receipt. Incredulous, the waitress looks to see who's listening, then leans in. *The same losers who broke you.*

On a Hot Night in August, M. & I Get Back Together for the First Time

1. *I see you're still a wanton thing,* M. laughs,
kisses my neck, tongues the salt.

He's always had my number.

2. *Hottest August on record,* swears Channel 7's weatherman,
Dallas Raines, sweat stippling his spray tan.

It's too hot for sex when the air-conditioner dies;
we drive instead to Topanga Beach in M's Fiat with the top down,
seeking a cool breeze.

3. M. is handy and we have this *arrangement.*

I think of him as a renewable resource.
He tells me I am the sun.

4. When we hit the beach the stars lick the ocean waves silver,
mica glistens on the sand. *A perfect night for lovers,* M. croons.

I'm just here for the dick, I say. A part of me likes to break his heart.

5. M. pulls me from the Fiat, fixes me against the hood, lifts my shirt.
My hot skin phosphoresces in the night.

Your tits, M. says, *are like two headlights.*
He wants to take them home.

6. I should know better.
But he smiles like he owns me.

And the wild moon rises, brazen, lecherous,
pins me in its beam like a klieg light.

Lola the Human Vagina at UC Medical School

For 25 years, Lola spread her legs
for the gynecology rotation,
decades of eager interns staring
into her nether regions
like it was virgin territory.

Beginning with the labia,
the attending physician explained their function,
pulled the lips apart like a flower,
then inserted the speculum,
so they could see all the way in.

Many had not seen a vagina
up close since birth.

Lola assured me she provided a service.
I make sure they see me
as a whole person, she said.

It paid well, and was almost respectable,
good money for a girl with no college.

I make a difference, she said proudly.
Not one of those young doctors
will ever look at a pussy
the same way again.

I try not to laugh.
I too tell myself lies.

When the famous poet's widower sidles up to you
at her memorial,

he'll ask if you're the same girl who used to live on Clinton Street, and
    weren't your sons
once friends? Old, with bushy brows and a scraggly beard, he'll be even
    more repellant.

You'll recall his fusty smell, how he'd push his way into your apartment,
sit too close to you on your couch, uninvited, stroke your hair.

He'll ask if you remember the handmade books he tried to sell you—
scribbled drawings, pages of ramblings disguised as poems, ink-
    splotched, unintelligible,

glitter escaping from the gaping pages onto your apartment's gray shag
    confusion;
how he almost coerced you into buying one, you, who could barely
    make rent,

who could barely afford cheap, Payless shoes for your growing boy.

Did I come on to you back then? he'll ask, gripping your arm so you can't
    escape.
He'll feign foggy, confused. When you answer *yes*, he'll smile, and say,

Yeah, well. In those days, I came on to everyone.

Clueless

Even a man who believes in nothing can find a girl who believes in him.
—*Joe, in* You, *American Thriller Series on Netflix (first episode, 2018)*

Even a man who believes in nothing can find a girl who believes in
him, but doesn't believe in herself. And if he's genius, he'll keep it that
way, keep her rudderless, shipwrecked, lost. I've been that damsel, and
it ain't pretty, the way he'll make the world constrict and loved ones
disappear, usurping them with an insatiable thirst for his approval, a
toxic longing so deep you can draw water. He'll drink it up, suck you
Sahara. Swear he's smitten while sexting the siren he's just met in the
checkout line at 7-Eleven. He'll count on your Cinderella complex, low
amour propre, and pathetic rescue fantasies. He'll be the one you've saved
yourself for—you'll be another notch on his gun. A hundred times I've
seen it, one "duped-girl" generation to another. You'd think millennials
would have a clue not to get drunk at parties or fall into bed with brag-
mouthed boys, to trust no one—let alone get in his car—and not to
throw themselves so willingly under life's callous bus. Don't these girls
watch Lifetime movies? *Law & Order SVU?* Don't they read YA novels
and listen to their moms? Some things don't change. Boys will be bad.
And girls won't believe it.

Things we lose are usually underneath something else

—for Benette R.

1.
I dream there is hair in my food.

In the morning, my lover says, "Yes,
there's a long hair in every dish you feed me."

A strand of myself in every serving—
and he eats it like a condiment.

2.
"Looks like the same M.O.,"
the detective says, examining our broken
pane, bent screen. "He likes you
long-haired girls."

3.
I find myself alone in the kitchen, eating
rice I don't remember cooking.

4.
"When was the last time we had any fun?"
my lover sighs.

5.
I mean, who are we when we enter
the Jacuzzi, and who are we
when we emerge?

6.
I dream there is food in my hair.
And gum. And a switchblade.

7.
"For the vast majority of people,"
my mother said just before she died,
"the thing that's going to kill you
is already on the inside."

Dress Rehearsal

I am trying on death like dresses.

The black, Donna Karan sheath beckons. Perfect for weddings, funerals,
   twice to court. Killer side slits.
Call it 38 Special.

The skimpy red "bandage" dress, tags still attached, dinner with Allison,
   a no-show.
Do I want to be dressed in devastation, found like that?
Call it death by misadventure.

The white silk shirtwaist with black polka dots Stella bought me at a
   discount
when she worked at I. Magnin. The back-stab stain that made it unwearable.
Call it exsanguination.

The blue velvet gown, ripped by Lorraine while tonguing *Veuve Clicquot*
   from my throat.
She left $300 on the nightstand with a note: "*Je ne regrette rien.*"
Call it strangulation.

The wraparound Diane Von Furstenberg I wore to give Anjelica
and her T-Bird the runaround.
Easy on/off. Like us, that molten L.A. summer
when I first slummed with girls.

Call it autoerotic asphyxiation.

The babydoll dress from my twenties I can't get rid of: white lace, pearl
   buttons,
straightjacket sleeves, mini-skirt flirting my reticent thighs.
Call it buried alive.

Domestic Violence

Knives cut both bread and throats, he warns, the stiletto's steel tip teasing my trachea. A love tap. I'm used to it. I don't react anymore; I bake. I knead, pound the dough instead of him. Each day when he leaves for court, those $2,000 suits camouflaging his viciousness, a brief reprieve. I envision his face in the smacked-down dough, push out the air pockets, dream of suffocation. I slap him, punch him, only to watch him rise. While he proofs, I look for loopholes, binge-watch *Forensic Files,* its endless stories of stymied desire, hour after hour of scheme and kill, each murder more gruesome, honed. I take notes, stick in a shiv to see if he's done, plot that he comes to a similar bad end. I shape loaves like alibis, knife-notched before they go into the oven, frenzied jabs and slices. I sharpen the blade, ready for his return. Like him, I'll never speak without a lawyer present.

1. Ode To My Husband's Back Hair

How it births just above his derrière, a dank profusion
of blackness, fuller as it reaches his waist,
climbs up either side of his spine like kudzu.

Lust, a determined furrow of dark confusion,
the spring and flatten of his pelt embraced;
the grip and tug of my exploring fingers.

How he lowers his sweet face down to me,
nuzzles my neck, his nose in my hair,
bare-back, silken, thick.

A dense forest tangles the slope of his shoulders,
grapples his neck. I starry night him in the shower,
soap his back, whorl his eager flesh,

Don McLean's *Vincent*,
sung straight-faced, an homage.

*(O Starry, Starry Night)

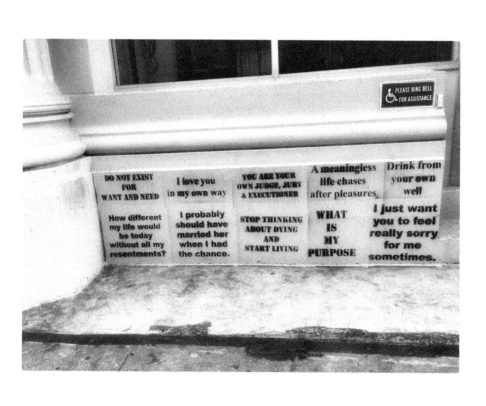

2. Ode To My Husband's Hitchhiker Thumbs*

Asked what about him I love best, I confess:
His thumbs. How they reach down, into me,
their hyper-extensibility, a jolt, a thunder bolt,

fresh from his double-jointed exploration,
curved inward, toward my center, the nub he rubs—
his heat-seeking digits for my clitoral amusement.

He's won the genetic lottery, two recessive
alleles determining a thumb's nature,
its bend-ability to please instead of tease.

How he slip-slides into me,
grabs my ass with dexterity,
holding firm, bent on pleasure.

I give him free rein, his thumbs
hitchhiking all over my landscape.

The Hitchhiker's Thumb is a thumb where the distal joint can bend as far backwards as 90 degrees. It is often referenced as a visual trait of genetic inheritance.

3. Ode To My Husband's Hernia Scars

She needs symmetry, my husband tells the surgeon,
pre-op, as if that explains everything. *She's an artist.*
He makes swashes through the air with his pointer fingers,

parallel, like two eyes, winking.
He's considerate of my POV, fellating his cock,
staring at his up-close groin.

Thoughtful like that, always looking ahead,
he knows the value of encouragement.
When the surgeon calls, post-op, she chuckles.

The incisions are identical, perfectly symmetrical.
Your spouse wanted me to reassure you, she says.
Once home, my husband lifts his shirt.

Wanna see my scars? Like they too, are art;
like they're every bit as sexy as back hair.

4. Ode To My Husband's Mouth

I trace his lips with my fingertips.
Generous portal, housing
his dexterous tongue.
When I suck it, he opens wide.

I push my body into his, hairy chest
tickling my breasts and belly:
heat-seeking, mesmerized,
spelunking each other's depths.

His tiny kisses follow me down,
earthquake at the back of my neck,
setting off fireworks, wet works,
a deep trembling.

Oh! How his lips respond to mine,
the lick and pull as he nibbles my clit,
my body's shudder, that hot-rush response
programed for his dining delight.

Gulp. Lap. Guzzle. Quaff.
A mouthful. A gobble. A canapé.

5. Ode To My Husband's Deviated Septum

When we're missionary, eye to eye,
his body wedged between my thighs,
and I look up into his face,
I see his nose is out of place.

The only time I wonder, why?
A biking mishap? Attempts to fly?
I ponder, from birth or accident?
A slip and fall on hard cement?

Then it hits me, when he goes "downtown"
it's his crooked nose that ruts around,
parts my labia, diddles my clit,
no reason to complain about it.

When asked, he shrugs, *I was born this way.*
I could have it fixed. — But why? I say.
I don't want to change you, not one bit.
Besides, I've gotten used to it.

I caress crooked cartilage, smooth the skin,
think of the places his nose has been.

6. Ode To My Husband's Heart

We call it *afterglow,* this reluctance
to uncouple, heartbeats synchronized,
in cahoots. We linger.

I caress his pecs, circle his left nipple
with my tongue, my ear close to his heart.
A human electrocardiogram, he ignites sparks.

When we fuck he is ventricles, arteries,
rimming my heart's surface, pumping pleasure
like oxygen into me, into us.

Webster defines it: "Young, easily cut beef, and
a sentimental heart can each be called tender."
If you're cooking, baby, make mine rare.

I hold my breath — will time to stop
in this heady space. Let us linger in his tenderness.

The Best Place to Cry in L.A.

It's only change, and change is good.
—Louise Hay

Grand Central Market was a good place to cry,

back when women wept over a fragrant cantaloupe,
ripped a pineapple's leaves from its body, testing for ripeness,
keened at the sight of a single, rotted lemon at the bottom of the bin.

Things change, my lover shrugs over *pupusas* at Sarita's Salvadorian.
Stop crying! Even when we're breaking up
he's telling me what to do.

You'll find someone better, he says. Like change is good,
and good men easy to find. Like Grand Central Market, gentrified,
is an improvement, the mom and pop's as dead as our love.

Nudged out by upscale eateries, artisanal cheese shops, oyster bars. No longer
a cheap respite from downtown's din. We locals priced out of the market.
Now it's a "tourist destination." *That's* something to cry about.

When I tell him I, too, can change, my lover suggests a complete renovation.
Lose some weight and you'll be more attractive, he prescribes.
Take a night class, improve your mind. For God's sake, stop being so needy!

He's done, but I dawdle at Sarita's counter, blue as their neon decor,
eat another *pupusa,* ponder my propensity for loss. *Stop crying!* my lover says,
heading for the exit. *No one cries here anymore. It's always sunny in L.A.*

Caged

Birds born in cages think that flying is an illness.
—Alejandro Jodorowsky

He loves me because I look like his mother at 30.
I discover her photo in a secret drawer,
the same rounded hips,

and dark, wavy hair,
her pale, off-the-shoulder blouse an exact
duplicate of one he's given me.

She has bigger breasts, deeper cleavage.
You eat like a bird! her son chastises,
passing me the cheesecake.

Suddenly it all makes sense.
Like when he cries *Mama!* in his dreams.
Awakens empty-armed. Abandoned.

He does not cry for me.

Shoved under our door, a flyer:
"If you find a dead bird, call 1-877-WNV-BIRD."
Lost between the bed and the mirror, I look and look.

He hides his obsession in a stack of magazines
in the bathroom. A blur of a girl, naked,
disappearing in a doorway. It could be his mother.

He locks the door.

Plump bird. Feathered nest.
Force-fed. *Fois gras.*

Fattened up for slaughter.

Someone's dinner. Someone's daughter.

When he hits me because I look like his mother,
he pulls back his fist, takes aim at her caged facsimile.
I hold perfectly still.

We both know he could never hit his mother.

Prey/Threnody

1. The Red-Tailed Hawk

picked off snakelets in the vacant lot,
stole eggs from the crows' nests on the bluff.

I'm unsure if for hunger or sport.

Like you, she took what she wanted.
Unlike you, she mated for life.

2. The Snake in the Grass

After you had your fill of me,
you retrieved your affection, packed your things.

The silence picked me clean.

Now, the red-tailed hawk bounces on the wire,
metronomes her beak like a hip hop star.

3. A Bird in the Hand

I've watched that hawk, snake in her mouth
like your snake has been in mine.

When did you fall out of me?

Last night, I saw Venus and the moon
duet in the starless sky. It could have been us.

4. Kamikaze

When the crows dive-bombed the hawk,
helpless to keep her from their nests,

she calmed. Unflappable.

The crows split the sky
with their laments, like me, distraught.

5. Mousy

The hawk, mouse in her beak,
circles overhead.

Alone at the window, I envy your next victim,

watch raccoons in pairs
cross the moonlit street like thieves.

At the Bar After His Reading, the Famous Poet Still Can't Recall My Name

But I think you're exceptionally fuck-able, he grins.

He doesn't remember:
How the booze flowed.
How the room spun.
How I fell into his bed.

Four martinis down, he nibbles a toothpick-speared olive,
gazes soulfully at my tits, as if they offer a clue.

I sidle up to his ear. *Here's a tip:*
It smelled like a Holiday Inn.

The famous poet adjusts his paunch,
eases another notch on his belt,
diddles with the bar food,
orders another round.

I slosh in the sea of his forgetfulness.

I want to tell him:
How it felt to be touched by fame.
How he never returned my calls.
How some nights, the only way I get off is to imagine his words.

How even tonight,
I can't keep my hands off him.

Little Shell/Big Ocean: The Awakening

1. Inside the shell: the girl. Almost 15, still submerged. She dreams ocean and desire until a boy swims out of her.

2. She's a bundle of suspense, her mother thinks. A handful. But the boy sees the girl, all her hunger. She has no mirror, does not yet know she is a siren.

3. Inside the shell: the girl. Her inner Mussorgsky. Her red bikini. Her demeanor a Mediterranean pink, the color of her sex, libido—a jitterbug of stars—thrown against her sky.

She plots her escape. Tests the latches. Her mother tests them, too.

4. The family astrologer charts the girl's course. Venus in Scorpio. Her Leo moon. The foreseeable future? *Mars in the 6th house and invasion.*

5. The little shell drifts. Treads water. Her mother wants to keep the girl safe. But she is exhausted & works full time.

6. Outside the shell: the boy. He's in over his head. His Circe is calling. The lure. The slosh and toss.

He buys a waterproof camera, infrared film to capture her.

7. The boy knows they are fated. Hard not to imagine jimmying the lock, their bodies colliding in the crashing waves, starlight, her briny coast glittering.

71

In the Drink

They've blockaded the beach. The parking lot, chained.
Forbidden. Like at your house. Changed locks. Restraining order.
Misunderstanding, I tell the judge. Why does no one believe me? I
sneak onto the empty pier where we'd stroll. Lie down, head vised
between two concrete posts. The murky water, just a splash below,
seems impenetrable as your indifference. I can make out seaweed
silhouetted against the dark, undulating current. Mackerel pulsing
silver. Waves soft-slapping against the pier, a lull so docile you'd never
imagine their rage. Kicked up by a storm, tossed by an aberrant Sea-
Doo. Like you, last night, a tempest I reduced to a squall. Cradled till
you realized it was me. Is this what you want? To fuck you and then
disappear? I ease my body between the posts, shimmy until I feel the
spray, my hair a tangle in the wind. I overheard you on the phone;
*If I could put a return label on her marked "broken" and ship her ass back,
I would.* Someone's killing peacocks, their bodies bob the harbor,
feathers broken, snapped.

The First Time I Commit Osculation

Strep. Mono. A broken heart. *Kissing leads to tragedy in flu season,*
my germaphobic mother swears, *especially kissing animals, and men are animals.*

Come back when you aren't a virgin, E. says. Perched on the couch at his studio
in Westwood, I refuse to leave. I want kissing and lift my smooth face to his,

begin at his neck, the bulge of Adam's apple an unscaled peak, my rapacious lips
at his throat. He tastes of salt and provocation. I lick the cleft of his chin.

He doesn't know I'm just 15, brazen with desire gleaned from bestsellers, misled
by implausible plot twists and their carnal resolution.

E. smacks of Marlboros and vacillation. Then he shrugs, nibbles my lips,
urges them apart. *You want this, right?* I guide his thick tongue down my throat.

Desire wildfires my body. But when I close my eyes I see my mother,
dousing my flames. As always, I am doomed to disappoint her.

Our love is a small motel in Van Nuys...

where nobody knows him. Our love is stolen, under wraps. Our love is no look/ no touch in the office; hook-up. *Amuse bouche.* Our love is black on white, savvy vs. eager, low light and dalliance. Our love is full-court lust between rough sheets on too-short afternoons. Our love is Willie's smallish cock and generous mouth, his agile fingers on my clit, his silver tongue down my throat. Our love tastes like chocolate. Our love is his 50-year-old body slipped between my coltish legs. Our love is his wife and my kid and just infrequent enough to keep it hot. Our love is a tutorial, a sweaty screw on the company dime, October afternoons when sales manager, Russ Fontaine, leaves early for Fontana to beat the traffic, his noxious urging to "go out and pump some sunshine," his motor-mouth at last put on hold. Russ can smell the sex on me and Willie. That look on his face, half confused, half jealous, nostrils flared, green eyes, feral. Look, our love is not love. Our love is autumn's shortened light. Often, when there's time, Willie coaches me on my sales technique. *You good with brothers,* he says. *And you got white folks down. But you a looong drink of water, baby.* He smiles, taking in the lank of me. *Asians?* he says. *You tower above them, and that ain't good. This is how you sell to Koreans,* he counsels, sitting me down on the side of the bed, so I look smaller and more respectful. Sometimes I imagine Russ in his company car, bumper to bumper on the 210 East and daydreaming of a threesome, while he inches home to his bed-ridden wife and "little" Russ, who at six has yet to utter a word, and who may or may not be his.

I Can't Afford to Complain

Joe Zamborelli sits across from me at his desk
at Line-X Spray-on Truck Bed Liners.
His fingers form a "V" in front of his lips,
while his lizard tongue darts in and out.

How're you doing today, babe?
You miss me?
His open leer, as always, half dare,
half invitation.

Each week I wonder what he'd do
if I took him up on it, if an old man like Joe
could even get it up, what with his gimpy leg,
saggy ass, and that pasta-gut spilling over his belt.

But a man can dream of oral sex
with the hot sales rep
who sits across from him week after week,
her low-cut blouse and sultry voice a magnet.

There's a thin line between compliment and assault.
I admit my complicity—I can't afford to complain.
I mean, how bad can it be? A blowout sale, a price change?
A whole new ad? I take his file from my briefcase.

Joe Zamborelli stares at my breasts,
licks his lips, considers his options.

And I, who work on straight-commission,
who have rent and daycare and a car payment due,
fix a smile on my own, fresh-painted lips,
tell him I'll take good care of him,

and how very, very happy
I always am to see him.

Recidivism

Tonight, I'm having drinks with my ex.
When I look for him at the bar,
his back will be to me. He will have less hair.

His ass will have spread.

When he tells me he's left his *blonde du jour,*
I'll swallow my deplorable glee,
tell him I've moved on.

But he'll commandeer me out of the bar,
stuff his resolve deep in my mouth,
make the sign of the cross.

Like a priest, he'll hide behind lust, then forgive *me.*

Look, each time he knocks me down, I right myself.
(I know which side I'm buttered on.)

He knows the limits; he hasn't killed me yet.

Tonight on the news: the word *battered,* used twice.
It's a sign.

I should have stayed home. Washed my hair.

When was the last time he hit you?
The intake worker will want to know.

Once, at fifteen, in a field in Camarillo, I picked raspberries,

ravaged the ruby rows,
juice-stained, and besotted

with the tall, fickle boy
who'd transported me there,

pretended to care.

I wanted him
to pick me.

But I was a dandelion;
he blew me off,

his rebuff a field of bitter fruit
that left me stunned for years.

Even now, at a party, when
someone asks what *field* I'm in?

I am always in *that* field,
ripe, stained,
waiting.

When I dream serpentine, 18 and lost
   ## in Istanbul again...

it's always the dream of the illusive snake ring at the Grand Bazaar. Heavy, rose gold, with emerald eyes. It gripped my finger. Would not let go. *It is for a man*, the turbaned merchant protested, tried to snatch it back. But I loved how it encircled, insinuated itself up to my knuckle. The way the orbs glinted, the enticement of its tongue. It spoke of a jeweled future. The merchant, impatient, wanted a decision, wanted too much. Money was tight. Adornment an invitation to be robbed in the confusion of Istanbul's perilous streets. It was a cruel century for a woman on her own. The ring, I told myself, was of no consequence, an extravagance, not a metaphor or a child. Yet, my life since that decision: rudderless. The abandoned ring a portend for each play-it-safe in my future, the uncertainty that accompanied every bad choice, each panicked dream. Tonight, I'll reconnoiter the bazaar, eighteen again, only smarter, self-possessed. The ring's snake eyes will flash an SOS through the labyrinth of narrow stalls, bolts of silk and brocade mingling with complicated carpets and incense and saffron and huge copper pots. I'll find it. I'll buy it and restart my life—erase each timidity, each dull mistake—the maze of shops an elaborate loss, a guilt trip, the scent of sandalwood in the air.

Old School, Part 2

It's 1970. I'm walking on Sunset when a man in a Ferrari offers me $500 for an hour of my time. Back then, that was a lot of money.

It's 1984 when my boss and her lover at the former Lincoln Heights jail are having sex standing up in a cell. C.Z.'s hand is under M.G.'s skirt. When asked to join in, I demur. I'm fired the week before Christmas.

It's 1978. In the noir director's Burbank hotel room, I audition for the lead. He rips my blouse in true tabloid style, the soundtrack for *Deep Throat* throbbing in the background. I decide to become a writer.

It's 1975 and John Crockett, né Gianni Carelli gets me high on coke, then makes love to my feet. Afterward he does Tai Chi by candlelight, slips me a C-note, calls me a cab. Every Wednesday for a year.

It's 1969. Eduardo drives me to the top of Topanga, parks on a cliff. After sex he whispers, *Querida, if I push you off the edge, no one will know.*

It's 1976 and John Crockett né Gianni Carelli begs me to have a three-way with Bobbie (the stripper we meet at the Body Shop). Afterward, John never calls me again. I begin dating Bobbie.

It's 1979 when I run into the noir director at The Dresden, a nubile young thing on each arm. I lean in: *Does he still like fucking to that Deep Throat soundtrack?* The starlets are startled, a moue of recognition on their lips.

It's 1990. Marcel E. trails me up the aisles of Pan Pacific Camera. *I'm shopping for a remote,* I say when he asks. *For self-portraits.* He licks his lips. *If I were you, I'd shoot myself every day!*

It's New Year's Eve 1987, when Richard F. takes me to Vegas. Up ten grand at the craps table, he hands me $500, pats me on the ass, says, *"Go play."* I go to Tiffany's, buy gold earrings.

It's 1977. Football star Eddie M. has non-consensual sex with me in my bedroom while my sister makes out with the fullback on my living room couch. We never speak of it again.

It's still New Year's Eve, Vegas, 1987. Richard F. takes me to the midnight show at the Hilton. Bill Cosby has never been funnier.

The Upper Hand

The man should always love you more than you love him.
—My mother

Why won't you let me get you off? my new lover asks.
How can I explain? I want to keep him.

If I let him pleasure me,
he'll know who I am.

That same night a couple, fighting below my window.
Her dirty mouth. Worse than the man's.

Goddam fuck you, I'll dance on your grave! she screams.
This is how love ends.

The question I ask myself:
Is that girl my twin?

The sickle moon hangs on a cloud,
the apex a stab, a howl; it throws no light.

I can't make out her face.

You can see something god-awful happened here,
my new lover says when he looks inside my head.

It's like he can read my thoughts.

Each night, the moon grows thinner,
more translucent. I mirror its waning,

its pull playing havoc with my tides. I don't want to feel.
I'm afraid I'll do something terrible,

like love him.

Heavy Weight, Clear Vinyl Shower Curtain ☆ ☆ ☆ ☆ ☆

I disturb your shower, fresh towels my excuse
to watch you stand beneath the spray,

water pouring off your hair, trickling down
your shoulders, beading your studly chest.

Fresh towels, the excuse for my eyes to linger
at your soaped-up cock, stiff in your hand.

I drop the towels, pull off my dress,
press myself into the vinyl, cool to the touch.

An inspired purchase, I think.

You reach for my breasts, slather your face between
the fogged, wet vinyl and me, mouth my nipples,

grip your cock harder, faster.

I reach between my legs for my clit,
finger myself to match your pace,
your hand a blur.

When your blue eyes close, I pull my fingers from inside me,
push aside the curtain, slide them into your mouth,
watch you lick your lips, grin.

Sometimes, we see right through each other.

Tomorrow I'll give the shower curtain a 5-star Amazon review,
as the seller, a mom and pop in Idaho, requested,
if I'm satisfied.

Guitar Man

—for D.S.

His heart was out of tune. Or maybe just unstrung. Too smart, too tall and socially awkward, his heart, he explained, went to college at sixteen, lunched alone, turned cold. He swore he thawed by moonlight, but only on those midnight walks with his thoughts and dog and never with me. His heart was a wah-wah pedal, mine, a muffled sob. Itchy for his fingers on its strings, his heart moaned in the dark, echoed from its bottomless sound hole. His fingers fretted down, capo strangling the neck, choking. When invited to the party, his heart proved unpopular, mumbled, danced alone. I wanted to save him but he stopped me at the door: "Man and his dog time," he said and shut me out. That I loved him even for a moment still astonishes. His heart played in someone else's band, angled for star turns, solos. It was a sign. When he left, he slung his heart over his shoulder, slept with it instead of me in his arms. Maybe you've seen him? His heart had a rosewood neck. Blue eyes. His heart chopped down women. His girlfriend. His wife, I'm told; his only daughter, tall as a tree.

Bad Mother

My boy died young.
I was a bad mother.
So was my mother.
My best excuse?
When she died young
I fell off the earth.
Think thud/careen not spiral.
Think death wish. Free-fall.
A blueprint, the way I see it.
Soupçon for self-loathing,
with a narcotic chaser.
(Lovers who'd sell me out
for a half-gram of coke.)
Not good choices.
My mother threw me to the wolves.
Loved my sister (the easier one)
and my brother more.
Died when I needed her most.
My dead boy sealed my fate.
My only one.
I pondered suicide.
Learned to police my head.
Mind over matter, my mother said.
But she never lost a child.
My near-fatal accident at twenty.
The day my little brother almost drowned.
Even then, my mother had two spare kids.
I should have had more.

The Famous Poet Apologizes for Not Coming on to Me Sooner

He presses into me a bit too hard when we embrace
after lunch at Octopus, where he spilled his most recent tryst

(the blonde who matched him drink for drink
on a day-cruise to Catalina, gave him a blow job on A-Deck).

I've been his daughter-confessor for years.

The famous poet updated me on his student-stalker, a fixture
since he broke her heart in 2015, who still leaves roses

on the hood of his vintage MG convertible,
scratches "I love you" in the paint with thorns.

The famous poet strokes my hair, tells me I'm beautiful.
You're every bit as desirable as the other women I've pursued, he says.

He asks why we've never hooked up before.
I tell him his life has too much drama.

He takes my words as a revelation,
my off-the-shoulder blouse, as an invitation.

The famous poet nuzzles my neck as we hug one last time.
I find décolletage particularly irresistible, he murmurs.

His lips get lost in my throat.

I remind him I'm married.
So am I, he says.

Thin-Skinned

You called it the "Winter of the Oranges," that February into March when our love was new, and the downtown Farmer's Market sold thin-skinned navel oranges for cheap. You'd grab our reusable bags and head for 5th Street, sampling each farmer's juicy segments before bringing home a ten pound sack. I'd never tasted such consistent sweetness—orange to orange, sack to sack, week to week—like nature had conspired to make every orange equal. Bursting they were—skin too thin to peel with fingers—they needed a sharp knife to slice them smartly into quarters or peel them whole, rind a single, perfect spiral, a three-way between peel, pith, and fruit. That winter you squeezed the juice into goblets, overflowing. You poured your love into me. But Spring came. The knife bled. Something stupid I said. You, and the oranges, turned bitter overnight.

82 Miles From the Beach, We Order the Lobster at Clear Lake Cafe

The neon flashes "Lobster" and "Fresh!"
The parking lot is crowded. We've been driving since dawn.

The lobster must be good here, you say.

The harried waitress seats us near the kitchen.
She's somewhere between forty and dead.

I show you the strand of her coarse, black hair
stuck between the pages of my menu.

Undeterred, you order the lobster for two.

I investigate the salad bar.

Yellow grease pools in the dregs of blue cheese dressing;
a small roach skims the edge.

Before the waitress can bring the clam chowder, I kick you under
the table.

I'm sorry, I say brightly. *We've changed our minds.*
I'm responsible for the look of defeat on her face.

As I head out, you stop and leave a twenty on the table.

I have never loved you more.

Porn on the Fourth of July

I like a man who can keep the party going, I say, nodding my head in sync with the actor's white ass as it pumps up and down. We're watching French porn, again, making fun of the way they use spit instead of lube. "French lube," we joke, unable to look away as the well-hung man hocks a loogie into an actress's lady parts. Aside from that I like the French—the men who stay hard for hours, the women who murmur *Oui! Oui! Oui!* with every thrust, like they can't get enough. Like me. Outside, too, it's steamy, the windows open to the sulfurous air. The night is rife with holiday pandemonium, and we can see the fireworks from here, golden chrysanthemums, shrieking crossettes and diadems, bursting. The neighborhood dogs staccato their non-stop howl, and when my lover ignites me I join them in a high-pitched chorus. Each day my love seduces me, finds new porn to tempt me. He knows what I like. Twosomes or threesomes. No tattoos. No bondage, brutality or handcuffs. In July he introduces me to Japanese metro porn. How the "schoolgirl" giggles behind her hand when the stranger lifts her skirt, salarymen surrounding the fornicating couple, oblivious. *You're a fool for love,* my lover says, and I say *Oui!* Outside, too, they're reaching the finale. Cherry bombs scar the dark. *Aaoooo!* That's us, going off like Roman candles, wailing louder than the dogs.

Hyena

I'm like a hyena, I get into the garbage cans. I have an insatiable curiosity.
—Leonora Carrington, painter

After Self-Portrait (Inn of the Dawn Horse) [1937–1938] by L.C.

That camel toe beckons from her white jodhpur pants like an
invitation, but of course, it's not. Instead, she extends her hand to
the hyena's toothy mouth, sits in the blue chair, the color of its eyes.
Out the window, a galloping white mare, forest-bound. *You're that
horse,* Leonora says. *I've set you free.* And she? *The hyena,* she sighs. She
paints herself as hermaphrodite, her elongated clit, that trio of dugs
hanging from her belly. Today when she reaches for me, I see who's
coming. Dark and cunning. Like her avatar. So unlike yesterday,
when we lay together in the high grass, the thin September light,
straw yellow, her face shading mine. *You're ravishing,* I said; she did
not believe me. I stroked the wild hair from her forehead, planted
kisses on her pulsing throat, tugged those white pants down past her
hips. Mercurial, intent on pleasure. How can I not adore her? I open
like a filleted animal. *Don't play me,* Leonora warns, when I gush over
the horse, delight in how she portrays me. *See the smudge, lower left?*
She points to a smear at the painting's edge where a figure once
lived. *I decided I didn't like her any more. It could have been you.*

The famous poet is silent for six months

and I'm afraid to call. Ever since
he failed to appear for lunch

at our favorite sushi bar,
ever since his final voicemail,

rambling even more than usual, how
he searched for me for hours,

couldn't find the restaurant,
had left his cell phone...somewhere.

The last time we met,
and I asked if he still wrote,

the famous poet was silent.
I can't remember, he finally confessed.

My breath caught.

Once, when I told him
he was better than Bukowski,

he looked at me like I'd blasphemed,
shook his head.

You can't mean that, he said.
But I did.

Regret Is a Dress to Be Buried In

All the dreams she had for her daughter, my grandmother crocheted into the dress, counted stitches. Filigree (happiness), embroidery (success), tatted lace (two solitudes, melded). The honey blond yarn a perfect match for my mother's hair, down to the shimmery gold strands woven through it.

Regret is cap sleeves, showing off her arms. Toned. All those years of ballet. The corseted waist, full skirt for dancing, the taffeta petticoat that gave her dress rustle and swish. The night of their 20th anniversary, how my mother twirled, dancing to Johnny Mercer's band, flaunting the dress, safe, she thought, in my daddy's arms.

So this is bliss? my mother sighed, sipped another vodka martini. Who knew cancer loomed in the lounge, lolled with the bartenders and servers on break, hid in the powder room, waiting to stitch itself into her colon, her stomach, her heart, an irregular mass—throwing off the count, crocheting caskets into everything.

Biting the Bullet

the girl is overdose.
her mother, a picnic
each Sunday on her grave.

the girl is eggshell—no,
the girl is soufflé.

dead meat, the boy
hangs himself
while housesitting.

his parents are a cut-short
European tour; why the rush—
dead is dead.

his mother is chasm.
she skids until memory
falls in.

Alzheimer's or grief?
not even the autopsy
knows for sure

but I do:
memory is bludgeon,
is dagger to throat,

is picnics in graveyards
will sink your boat.

this is what I know to be true:

either you bite the bullet
or the bullet bites you.

The God for Broken People

There is a god for broken people.
—Roxanne Gay

This is the god for the second rate, the one who waylays you at the party, plies you with bourbon, fucks you in the kitchen, makes you walk home in the rain. This god shines in the run-off. This god hustles the night. This god mines the maimed, culls emotional cripples off the top like cream. This god is a shape-shifter, a dumpster diver, the god who loiters at the corner of Dolorosa & Despair. This god drinks alone. The god for broken people trolls the city for discards, marries the exploited with the lost. This god sweeps up the miscreants, gusts their darkness into night. This is the god of no hope. No money. This god has your back when you backslide. This god bets on you to fail, hides in your broken places. This god is willing to wait. When you're ready to surrender, remember: this is your last, best chance. This god will not stick by you, won't give you false hope. This god will kill you. Or save you. Choose.

ACKNOWLEDGMENTS

Epigraph for "She Says Stalker/He Says Fan" is by Rita Dove, quoted from "Canary" from her fourth book of poems, Grace Notes (W. W. Norton & Company, 1991).

Many of the poems in this collection were published, or are forthcoming, in these venues:

A-Minor Magazine	When I dream serpentine, 18 and lost in Istanbul again...
Anomaly Literary Journal	Pas de Deux
Blank Rune Press	Lola the Human Vagina at UC Medical School
Blood Orange Review	I Audition for the Belly Dancer Job While My Pure-bred Siamese Lily Gets Laid
Blood Orange Review	Thirst
Carbon Culture	For Mary, My College Roommate, Who Sells Drugs & Wants to Be a Porn Star
Carbon Culture	On a Hot Night in August, M. & I Get Back Together for the First Time
Chiron Review	Prey/Threnody
decomP	Things we lose are usually underneath something else
Diaphanous	Caged

Gyroscope Review	Why We Didn't
Harbor Review	Power Play
Mudfish Magazine	Dress Rehearsal
The Pedestal Magazine	Hyena
Petrichor Magazine	After the breakup, I retreat into Sappho at my usual diner
Pirene's Fountain	Poem for the Girl Who Wanted to Stop Time
Plume	Sweet Tooth
Pratik	The Famous Poet Sexts Me While His Wife's Asleep
Pretty Owl Poetry	Our love is a small motel in Van Nuys…
Rag Queen Periodical	Little Shell/Big Ocean: The Awakening
Rat's Ass Review	6 Odes To My Husband's Body Parts
Rattle, Persona Poems	Tonight at last call, J. calls me his Brown Liquor Girl again,
San Pedro River Review	She Says Stalker/He Says Fan
San Pedro River Review	The God for Broken People
Slipstream	82 Miles From the Beach, We Order the Lobster at Clear Lake Cafe

Slipstream	Midnight in the Backyard of Lust and Longing
SWWIM	At the Party, the Famous Poet Goes Too Far With the Latest Sweet Young Thang
SWWIM	When the famous poet's widower sidles up to you at her memorial,
The American Journal of Poetry	Bad Mother
The American Journal of Poetry	Recidivism
The American Journal of Poetry	When I asked him to turn me on he said:
The Ramingo's Porch	Heavy Weight, Clear Vinyl Shower Curtain ☆☆☆☆☆
Tinderbox Poetry Journal	When your stepdaughter warns you not to let her roommate's cat escape...
Vox Populi	Thin-Skinned
Willawaw Journal	After the Restraining Order Expires, M. Begs Me to Meet Him for Lunch

THANK YOU

I'm indebted to my posse of extraordinary poets; Cynthia Atkins, Michelle Bitting, Chanel Brenner, Ellaraine Lockie, and Bill Mohr for their edits, encouragement and love. Gratitude to my sister, Debra, for her generosity and fierceness, and for always saying yes. Thanks to my remarkable publisher, Raymond Hammond, for believing in my work. Kudos to my beloved city of Los Angeles for the inspiration. And thank you to my darling Fancher, who knows me so well and loves me still.

—*Alexis Rhone Fancher, Los Angeles, CA, February 2023*

CPSIA information can be obtained
at www.ICGtesting.com
Printed in the USA
BVHW041954190323
660752BV00004B/21